What People Are Saying About

The Daughter-in-Law Rules

"Next to   nay be the
best wed<

Tim Bete
e Parenting

"The Dau   ou will find
funny anc

Lynne Klippel
founder, www.BusinessBuildingBooks.com

"I love this book! *The Daughter-in-Law Rules* is delightful with an unapologetic truth about a tremendously complex relationship constellation."

Dr. Jackie Black, PH.D.
relationship expert, coach and author, *Meeting Your Match*

"The DIL Rules is the Bible for *all* daughters-in-law and daughters-in-law to be! Sally provides an entertaining and funny, yet practical and down-to-earth guide to dealing with the mother-in-law."

Joseph Ghabi
founder, www.FreeSpiritCentre.info

"Read this book today if you want to learn how to turn your biggest naysayer into your strongest advocate!"

Patrick Snow
best-selling author, *Creating Your Own Destiny*

"Sally's Shield's book is a refreshingly funny and honest, yet kindhearted perspective on an issue that no doubt perplexes countless women worldwide. There are a MIL-lion reasons to read!"

Scot McKay
professional dating coach and founder, X & Y Communications
www.DeserveWhatYouWant.com

"I am buying this for my daughter-in-law— how else is she going to be able to cope with me? "

Joan Bechtel
co-author, *Motherhood Confidential*

"*The Daughter-in-Law Rules* provides confidence building, fire extinguishing, relationship harmonizing anecdotes to an often challenging marriage experience that will help you keep the peace and create more love."

Karinna Kittles-Karsten
best-selling author, *Intimate Wisdom, The Sacred Art of Love*

"This handy tongue-in-cheek guide is amusing, entertaining and practical. A must-have for *all* daughters-in-law—especially those with M.I.L.D.E.W. (mothers-in-law do everything wrong)!"

Liz Bluper and Renée Plastique
co-authors, *Mothers-In-Law Do Everything Wrong: M.I.L.D.E.W.*

"This is the handbook everyone has been waiting for! Finally, a How-To that will insure success with even the most challenging of mothers-in-law—because as we know, sometimes talking is just not enough. Follow this advice, and you will experience a lifetime of wedded bliss!"

Susan Page
author, *Why Talking is Not Enough*

"Wishing you had married an orphan? Forget Valium, read the *Daughter-In-Law Rules*! If you follow even half of Sally Shield's MIL "management" advice, you'll save yourself years of frustration, anger and anti-depressants!"

Lisa Earle McLeod
syndicated newspaper columnist and author, *Forget Perfect* and *Finding Grace When You Can't Even Find Clean Underwear*

"I loved every minute of this book! Sally illuminates a classically delicate relationship with such a zesty playfulness that instead of cringing I was laughing. Easy to follow advice, coupled with wit and humor, I finished *The Daughter-in-Law Rules* in one sitting!"

Susanne Paynovich
aquatic exercise specialist, and founder, www.WaterGym.com

"Sally Shields is an especially talented and superb author with a terrific sense of humor. I would recommend this book to any married woman or soon to be married bride!"

Bob Burg
author, *The Go-Getter* and *Winning Without Intimidation*

"The DIL Rules rule! Sally Shields has hit on every problem I've faced with my MIL and then some. Now all I have to do is follow her sage advice—but do I really have to ask how she's feeling???"

Deb DiSandro
humor speaker and author, *Tales of a Slightly Off Supermom: Fighting for Truth, Justice and Clean Underwear*

"A great gift for any long-suffering or soon to be daughter-in-law. Slip one in your mother-in-law's Christmas stocking too. After all, as Sally reminds us, she really must be a great mother—you fell in love with her son didn't you?"

Janet Beckers
founder, WonderfulWebWomen.com

"What you focus upon expands based on the Law of Attraction, and that is what will happen when you apply this approach. With Sally Shield's 101 ways, you will improve your relationship with your MIL tenfold!"

Christy Whitman
best-selling author, *Perfect Pictures*, certified Law of Attraction coach and creator of www.7EssentialLaws.com

"With these 101 essential strategies, you can experience personal growth in 101 ways as well. Not only did Sally Shields positively transform her relationship with her mother-in-law, but she became an Amazon.com best-selling author at the same time! Now that's growth!"

Manny Goldman
author, *The Power of Personal Growth*
and founder, www.PersonalGrowth.com

"Sally Shields takes what appears to be a very difficult relationship and turns it around into one comprised of respect and love by way of some wonderful and easy to implement techniques. May we all follow her example to be loving, kind, generous, openhearted, sensitive people. Well done, Sally!"

Tulum Dothee
certified educator and founder, www.MindfulParentingTips.com

"This book is truly brilliant! MIL 101 should be a mandatory course in universities and even high schools across the country. Thank you Sally Shields for your witty and wonderful book!"

Kelly Sullivan Walden
author, *Discover Your Inner Goddess Queen*
and *I Had the Strangest Dream*

The
Daughter-in-Law
Rules

101 *Surefire* Ways to Manage
(and Make Friends with) Your Mother-in-Law!

Sally Shields

Outskirts Press, Inc.
Denver, Colorado

The Daughter-in-Law Rules
101 *Surefire* Ways to Manage (and Make Friends with) Your Mother-In-Law!
All Rights Reserved.
Copyright ©2008 Sally Shields
V7.0
Cover Photo ©2008 Jupiter Images Corporation. All rights reserved—used with permission.

Outskirts Press, Inc.
http://www.outskirtspress.com

ISBN: 978-1-4327-1837-4

Library of Congress Control Number: 2008921231

Outskirts Press and the "OP" logo are trademarks belonging to Outskirts Press, Inc.

PRINTED IN THE UNITED STATES OF AMERICA

This book is dedicated to my mother-in-law

Contents

Acknowledgement _____

A Very Special Thanks to
Audrey Welber

Why I Wrote
The Daughter-in-Law Rules

Your MIL is coming! Your MIL is coming! As your husband announces that his mother is due to arrive in a couple of hours, your hands sweat and your heart begins to palpitate as you quickly try to neaten and straighten the house to perfection. HELP! Can you possibly live up to her standards? Will anything you do be to her satisfaction? Why does the mother of your beloved always cause such fear and trepidation? And when that bell finally rings, you open up the door with a gargantuan smile. With the most genuine welcome you can muster, you gush, "Hi MOM! How was your trip?" Without skipping a beat she barks back, "The traffic was *horrible*—took me two hours to get here. My neck is KILLING me, Take my bags in. You look like @#$%^*! Better take some Dayquil. Where are my little angels?"

You sigh heavily as you pick up her suitcase and purse your mouth into a tight-lipped smile. There *has* to be some magic technique for dealing with mothers-in-law! After all, almost every wife you know has issues with hers... EUREKA! A set of strategies! What if you had a crystal ball, and you could anticipate all of your MIL's quirky comments in advance? What if there was a method to mitigate her faultfinding ways *ahead* of time? You dream of being prepared for all the curve balls that come hurtling your way—what if you could deflect the bulk of them, and be at ease when she walks through the door?

And suddenly you remember that there's hope—you'll go and re-read *The Daughter-in-Law Rules*! You straighten your posture and feel a new empowerment for battle. And while you offer Mom a nice cup of tea, that old joke comes to mind: "How do you get to Carnegie Hall? Practice, practice, practice!!!"

I spent many an hour on the long rides back from the Midwest trying to get my husband to feel my anger, hurt and frustration about his mother's irritating behaviors and verbal barbs. But after several years of having the same old conversations with him about this issue, I realized the bond between a mother and her son is impenetrable and there was no way in Kalamazoo I was going to get him to take sides. I can't tell you how many times my husband said to me, "If you can't find a way to get along with my mother, then we might as well just call it quits!" There seemed to be no end to this troublesome cycle! I now know that he wasn't saying this to hurt me, but rather out of a deep fear that the two most important women in his life would not be able to get along. I eventually figured out that *I* had to be the one to change my viewpoint or this exasperating dynamic would continue or worsen.

I knew I had to take matters into my own hands, as I loved (and love now more than ever!) my husband dearly. It was an essential move, coming up with these DIL Rules! So whenever a bothersome incident would pop into my head, I jotted down longhand, on the back of napkins and any other scraps of paper I could get my hands on, a new strategy for dealing with my MIL. I started writing down all the bloopers that I seemed to make over and over with her and created a rule and a solution to deal with each and every one—from household matters to beauty techniques, to handling her lovely (and oh-so-appreciated) advice about to how to deal with my children!

Though this exercise started off as a tongue-in-cheek coping mechanism, once I began putting a few of these rules into practice, I noticed that my MIL's attitude started to shift. I began to see her softer, gentler, more agreeable side, and realized that she actually wanted to be quite helpful and kindly towards me. I began to really like her—a lot, in fact! I thought that if she and I could actually have a non-confrontational, even pleasant rapport, (which has now turned into a loving bond), then these rules really have something to them, and maybe I could help to save other young wives needless contention by letting them in on my little secret!

The point of *The Daughter-in-Law Rules* is to help you stay one step ahead of your mother-in-law. It won't be easy at first. (When the going gets tough, remember, you are younger and hipper than she is, but most importantly, you have her son!) You'll notice that as you start to apply these calculatingly affable defenses you will no longer be looking for her approval. You will begin to coexist peacefully with her, and experience smooth sailing with your husband too, because the two most important women in his life are getting along.

Now let's go and have some fun!

PART 1:
The Newlywed

Rule#1: _____

Call Your MIL "Mom"

*A*t the inception of your marriage your MIL may take it upon herself to inform your husband, "I only have ONE rule—that she calls me MOM!" As hard as it is getting used to, do it anyway. You will soon adjust to it and eventually you may actually enjoy having a second mom. It will also help to remind you who's the boss. (Hint: It isn't you!)

Rule #2: _____

Call Your MIL Regularly

 ou can keep it short, but if you're super-busy, aim for getting her machine, like when you know she'll be at Bingo.

Rule #3: _____

Tell Your MIL What a Great Job She Did As a Mother

And truly mean it! After all, you chose to marry her son! This will most likely bring her to tears.

Rule#4: _____

Frequently Ask Your MIL How She's Feeling

Make sure you take the time to notice how much your MIL's back has been bothering her recently, and be extra helpful around the house at these times. You are slowly becoming aware of the fact that Mom has a proclivity for stating the opposite of things you say, so when you offer her your sincerest sympathy, she might even reply that she's feeling well! But keep in mind that it's not easy getting old and aches and pains can make even the best of us ornery as all get go. And as an added touch, offer to accompany your MIL on doctors visits whenever possible.

Rule#5: _____

Compliment Your MIL's Looks — Often!

Your MIL can be self-conscious just like you are, so make sure you let her know how pretty, thin, healthy, and young she looks. Say what flattering outfits she wears, occasionally asking if you can borrow a certain item of clothing or a purse. Mention that you absolutely love her hairstyle, even if she's wearing a hairpiece (especially if she's wearing a hairpiece). In fact, go out and get yourself a hairpiece and you too will appreciate the benefits of "fake hair!"

Rule #6: _____

Mark Your MIL's Birthday, Anniversary and Mother's Day On Your Calendar and Send Her Cards

On each of these occasions, pick out a Hallmark with the most heartfelt sentiments but make sure your husband signs it too. Receiving a note solely with your handwriting on it will surely disappoint your MIL into thinking that her son may have forgotten her special day. Better yet, have him pen the note from the both of you. And be sure to call 1-800-FLOWERS well in advance so that those roses are sure to arrive on time, not three days after the fact—no, no, no!

Rule #7: _____

Be As Unassuming As Possible Around Your MIL

The worst thing you can do is be sarcastic or standoffish with your MIL. Make sure to be humble as pie or she may mistakenly get the wrong impression and say something to the effect of, "You act so high and mighty, like you're *better* than everyone else!" thus making you feel like something the dog dragged in. Rather, opt for the alternative and channel your 8th grade drama teacher. Over-affect everything from gracious guest to light and wispy wallflower.

Rule #8: _____

Try Not To Get Defensive With Your MIL

For instance, if you happen to be talking aloud to yourself mumbling something like, "Where the heck are the new tea bags I just bought?" your MIL may mistakenly think you are accusing her and pounce with a self-protective, "Don't look at *me*! *I* didn't do it!" Rather than rolling your eyes and glancing askew while uttering defensively, "Look, I didn't say YOU took them, did I?" do a 180 and rather reply with an airy, "Oh, I am just *so* forgetful these days! Just last week I found my keys in the fridge—I must be losing my mind!" Simply take a deep breath, locate your missing item and make yourself a nice cup of chamomile. And be sure to graciously offer your MIL her choice of beverage as well.

Rule #9: _____

If Your MIL Criticizes You, Be Objective

If your MIL tells you your hair looks better the *other* way, enthusiastically thank her mentioning how difficult it is to be objective about oneself. Then style it the OTHER way while visiting. Of course you can change it back when she leaves, although she very well might be right about this one. So be open to the possibility that Mother knows best!

Rule#10: _____

Follow a Compliment By Your MIL With a Self-Deprecating Comment

When every now and then your MIL does dole out that rare, yet appreciated accolade such as, "You look good in that dress," remember to follow all flattering remarks with humble self-deprecation, like so: "Oh thanks—I was going for a particular look but I'm really not sure I succeeded very well at all. Thanks for noticing!" And be truly glad she did!

(On Advice)

Rule #11: _____

Frequently Ask Your MIL
For Her Advice

Tell your MIL how much you value her opinion, but make sure she doesn't overhear you querying the same thing of someone else, since you don't ever want her to feel invalidated. She might then tearfully proclaim, "Well, I don't know why you ask *me* anything. You always go and get your answers elsewhere anyways!" It's important that your MIL knows that her guidance is special. But keep in mind that it may be best, at least until you master the approach outlined herein, if the subject matter remains on the simple and inconsequential side. As well, let your MIL know how much you appreciate her recommendations, even when it is unsolicited (especially if it is unsolicited!). While suffering from the common cold, for example, even while your MIL is doling out a sympathetic remark or two, be prepared for it to be accompanied by her unique brand of tact: "You look like @#$%^&!!" She may then suggest the latest over-the-counter pharmaceutical. Thank her profusely, but before taking it make sure that it isn't one that is on the list of medications to avoid due to its strong anticholinergic and sedation properties. Then promptly go to the health food store and stock up on lots of Airborne, Emergen-C, Zinc and Ecchinacia.

Rule #12: _____

...but DON'T Ask Her Opinion on Professional Matters!

If you're contemplating starting a home-based business, for example, try not to end a sentence with, "What do you think?" as this will give your MIL the wide-open opportunity to declare something like so: "Oh, I would NEVER do that! What a waste of time and money!" However, if you do try to get her endorsement for that new Multi-Level marketing opportunity and she downplays your enthusiasm, simply say, "Wow, you are *so* right. I hadn't thought about that side of things before— I'm not going to give this crazy scheme another thought!" Then, buy all her birthday and holiday gifts with the 40% discount you get from your new business. Even better, wrap up all the stuff you win from your super-starter incentive bonus packages and regift 'em to the relatives at Christmastime!

(On Interests)

Rule#13: _____

Do Not Expect Your MIL to Share Your Interest in Movies

Since you are now fully aware that your MIL regularly voices the opposite opinion of much of what you say, like or do, change the course of things with a simple teach-by-example strategy and follow her up with a corroborative statement or two. For instance, while watching a James Bond marathon on TNT during the holidays, Mom may disdainfully decree, "How can you watch those silly movies over and over again? How *incredibly* boring. You've seen one, you've seen 'em all! And that new Bond there—what the heck's his name? I hear he's gay as a daisy! He looks like a dork too, and his body ain't that hot, 'neither!" Okay, Riiiiiight! So, rather than launching into a diatribe about how each film is an epic masterpiece chock full of brilliantly-casted star ensembles and jaw-dropping action scenes, (not to mention the drool quotient from Sean Connery to Daniel Craig), reasonably respond with a rapid, "That is just SO true! I can't tell the difference between Roger Moore and Pierce Brosnan, and all the plots are *exactly* the same!" (Then fluff up your pillow and hide the remote.)

Rule#14: _____

Do Not Expect Your MIL to Share Your Interest in Music

For example, if your MIL happens to be watching an episode of "American Idol" and someone who you think is God-awful comes on be prepared for her to yell out, "She can *sure* sing—I guarantee you she will be in the top ten!" Or a really great, professionally bound vocalist will perform and Mom may comment only about her lack of fashion sense: "What the hell's she wearing? Jesus, it's like she just stepped out of a homeless shelter! And can't they do something about her hair? She looks like Sergeant Pepper on acid!" Or Liza Minnelli may be guesting on some talk show promoting a new book or such, and just as you're ready to wax poetic on how you so respect her long, distinguished career and what a mark she's made in music, stage and screen, out comes a screeching, "Oh that @#$%^&* Daughter of Dorothy! Why doesn't she get a regular haircut!" Make sure you zealously concur with each and every one of her assessments, but try to stifle your inescapable giggles like a schoolgirl passing notes.

Rule #15: _____

Do Not Expect Your MIL To Join Your Book Club

If you happen to be reading a really intriguing book, you may mention something to the effect that your MIL might be interested in it after you get through to which she may respond, "You *know* I don't like to *read*, [insert your name here]!" Try to remember that not EVERYONE enjoys studying the latest UFO abduction case or new evidence pointing to spiritual survival after death.

Rule #16: _____

Strive to Keep Quiet When Watching Quiz Shows With Your MIL

Try not to shout out too many questions or answers correctly while watching "JEOPARDY!" or "Who Wants to Be a Millionaire" with your MIL. You don't want to feel self-conscious for letting your grasp of the English language, trivia, literature and general knowledge ranging from geography to astronomy accidentally slip in and make your MIL feel awkward if she did not have the same educational goals as you and your family. So let Mom be the one to answer the questions and when she nails 'em, marvel at her knowledge! She'll be certain to surprise you, however, especially in the category of pop-culture as the E Channel is often running full-time during the day. You can soak up a lot of information while bustling about the house cooking and cleaning, that's for sure!

Rule #17: _____

Don't Let Your MIL Sour Your Soap

*Y*ou may enjoy watching a particular soap opera now and then and take the opportunity to tune in when visiting your MIL. Be prepared for her to give you her two cents on the matter: "It's about time you gave up that stupid show—what a bunch of @#$%^! And some of them actors are downright Butt-Ugly, too! Nothing happens on them things anyways. I saw that show 20 years ago and that old millionaire there—you know the one with the silver hair? He had that same gosh-darned hair back then too! Well, he should be about ready to keel over by now. That show would be a heck of a lot better with him ten feet under, that's for *darned* sure!" Just temper her with at tepid, "Yes, you are *so* right... who has time for silly time-wasters like "All My Children" anymore? Not me! Far be it for me to be watching TV anyway—I have a husband to take care of! He certainly needs my attention at every moment. I even like to watch him when he's napping, sometimes!" Then go online and read all your recaps. And when you get home, kick back and enjoy a bout of boxing between Erica (La Lucci) Kane and Adam Chandler. Well, at least your MIL got one thing right—you probably haven't missed much!

Rule #18: _____

Do Not Expect to Have Your Favorite Shows TIVO'd When Your MIL is Visiting

As soon as that little red button pops up, your MIL may straight away grab the remote and instantaneously change the channel to a Western of the week. "YOU TWO NEED 2 TV'S!" she'll caterwaul, while reaching for a bag of popcorn, extra butter, leaving you thoroughly bereft as you mourn the passing of this week's episode of "LOST." Just go online and download it later. That's why your husband got you that 22" monitor for Christmas, right? Besides, you might even find that John Wayne was actually hot in his day! Make yourself a bag of popcorn too, (fat free no salt) and chomp away to your heart's content.

(On Gift Giving)

Rule #19: _____

Better to Tell Your MIL You're An X-Large

If your MIL calls to ask what size you are, safer to say that you're feeling really self-conscious about your weight and she'd better get an X-large just to be safe. Do not respond with Medium (or heaven forbid Small) or you'll invariably end up with an XXL garment at Christmastime. However, by telling her that you are an X-Large, you will ensure that you receive *at least* a Medium. But if you happen to be feeling a little on the plus side, make a new-year's resolution, stick to your diet and go to the gym. And if you do end up with an XXL garment or two, no worries, just wear it as jammies!

Rule #20: _____

Save Gifts From Your MIL
For At Least a Year

When your MIL bestows a gift upon you, make sure you display it prominently in your home, or wear it a lot when she arrives. If it happens not to be quite your cup of tea, don't make the mistake of getting rid of it prematurely. There is nothing more humiliating than not being able to produce whatever it may be upon inquiry due to over-hasty regifting. Keep the item in question for a minimum of at least four seasons.

Rule #21: _____

Send Thank You Notes To Your MIL

No matter what the gift, make sure you send your MIL a handwritten note to express your appreciation. But just in case she says, "Whatever you do, DON'T send me Thank You cards! We're *family*!" a simple phone call will suffice. And be happy that she finally considers you part of the family unit!

Rule #22: _____

Let Your Husband Be The One to Pick Out Gifts For Your MIL

Don't take it personally if your MIL doesn't like the presents you give her. Although you may have thought yourself to be very clever and selected something that you are sure *anyone* would have loved (who wouldn't?!) don't be surprised if you find out that the yearly *Star Magazine* subscription that you've been renewing in Mom's name for the last several years has been making it's way over to the hair salon—unread! (How unimaginable is THAT!) Just transfer the remaining issues over to yourself. The very best way to handle gift giving with Mom is to let your husband do the buying. Even if the responsibility of holiday shopping usually ends up on your shoulders, give him the assignment of this one single thing—it'll be worth your while to make sure he follows through!

PART 2:
On House and Home

(At Your House)

Rule #23: _____

Before Your MIL Comes For a Visit, Make The Bed With Her Linens and Put Her Towels In the Bathroom

If your MIL enjoys storing her own linens, pillows, blankets, comforters and towels at your house for use when she visits, make sure you have them ready and put them out upon arrival. Condense them nicely in some shrink-wrap material and place them in a box under the bed upon her departure.

Rule #24: _____

Put Up the Household
Items Your MIL Brings Over

If your MIL supplies you with things to improve your home such as curtains, rugs, rags and potters, set them about and thank her graciously. If they are not to your liking, simply remove them after she leaves. Put them in a special box labeled, "my favorite household items" and take them out again before her next visit. If she gives you Christmas decorations, put them on your tree when she comes. There is nothing bothersome about Christmas decorations! That's one less thing you have to remember to do during the holiday season. Enjoy them!

Rule #25: _____

Always Empty Your Fridge Before Your MIL Comes To Visit

Your MIL may arrive with a giant car-show sized cooler replete with Wonder Bread Hot Dog Buns and Oscar Meyer Dogs, Tupperwares full of Sloppy Joes, macaroni salad, and of course, a Ziploc of iceberg lettuce with jars of her very own homemade dressing. If there's no room in your refrigerator, she'll simply jostle your stuff to the side, perhaps even knocking it to the floor like so: "You just have your stuff piled all up in there! You need a bigger @#$%^&* fridge!" Rather than witness your tofu stir-fry strewn all over the tiles, make sure you keep a shelf or two wide open for your MIL and her stockpile of provisions.

Rule #26: _____

Agree With Your MIL About
What a Disaster Your Home Is

o everything you can to make your house as neat as possible before a visit, even if it means hiring a cleaning service. In the process of neatening up, however, you might pick a room in which to deposit the extraneous clutter so the rest of your dwelling appears sparse and orderly. Inevitably, this will be the area that your MIL finds first, promptly informing you what a *complete* catastrophe your home is. (Unfortunately, she does have a point there!) Thus, utilize the technique of pre-emptive apologizing—beat Mom to the punch and tell her you are going to sign up for one of those home-improvement shows on HGTV such as "Before and After," "Designers' Challenge" and "What's With That House?"

Rule #27: _____

Do Not Expect Your MIL to Appreciate Vegetarian Food

You may be discussing a wonderful meal that you just enjoyed at a new vegetarian restaurant that just opened up in your neighborhood. You are marveling at all the wondrous properties of soy from the health benefits to its ability to resemble chicken and fish in taste and texture, to which your MIL may remark, "That there stuff is *disgusting*!" Try to remember that Mom, having lived in the same town on the same street all her life, may have had a narrower repertoire of dining possibilities than your cosmopolitan self. Counter with a compliant, "That is *too* true. Usually I end up going to get a slice about a half-hour later anyway. That vegetarian stuff just doesn't fill you up like a good pizza!"

Rule #28: _____

... so Better to Order Out When Your MIL Comes to Visit!

*A*nd certainly do not bother creating a meal, as your MIL will most likely not be accustomed to your type of food. The amount of effort you put into producing it will be inversely proportionate to her reaction. For example, you may spend two days preparing a wonderful feast: penne with pesto, pine-nuts and sun-dried tomatoes, green salad with caramelized walnuts, pear and gorgonzola cheese, spicy black bean dip with onions and garlic, tabouli salad with garbanzo beans and avocado. As you proudly announce, "Dinner is served!" the doorbell may simultaneously ring to the tune of DOMINO'S. So save yourself the trouble and order a couple of large pepperoni pies, or simply take Mom out to the local diner.

Rule#29: _____

Offer To Do the Laundry
When Your MIL Comes to Stay

If your MIL laments that you have too many stairs, offer to do the wash. Otherwise she might blurt out a statement such as, "I hate your house!" as her one-floor modular is certainly far easier on her arthritic joints. Make sure to use lots of fabric softener, though, asking her which brand she prefers. Help her as much as possible with the running up and down the steps. Bring her Lipton tea in the morning and Lay's in the evening (preferably Salt & Vinegar Artificially Flavored Potato Chips to be specific).

Always Make Sure To Close the Top Cabinets in the Kitchen

Even if you are multi-tasking like an octopus—hustling about preparing a dinner of salad and spaghetti, speaking to HOME DEPOT on the phone regarding that new siding for the house while trying to do your hair and nails and simultaneously getting dressed for an evening class at the Learning Annex, make sure you close the kitchen cabinet doors or your MIL may holler, "Make sure you close those cabinet doors, Missy! I've already cracked my head TWICE on them things!" OH NO! First, make sure she's all right, then follow up with some damage control like so: "Oh my gosh, I'm SO sorry about that, Mom! Are you okay? I *do* have a tendency to forget those matters. In fact, an old roommate once pointed out the very same fault in me many years ago. Seems I still haven't learned my lesson—I'll sure try to remember better from now on!" (Oops...well at least your MIL has a hard head!)

Rule #31: _____

Let Your MIL Help You With Your Landscaping

If your MIL wants to pick out shrubs for your garden or bulbs for the flower boxes, tell her how fabulous her selections are. Do not wrinkle your nose or peer disapprovingly in your husband's direction or she may likely exclaim, "You are just SO contrary, and I'm not the *only* one who thinks so!" Rather, let Mom pick out the curiously interesting bushes. After all, she does have a lot more experience than you do in these matters, and remember, you really need to pick your battles. You might even be pleasantly surprised when they grow in as to just how nicely they blossom and bloom! But if you absolutely must, simply replace them with your own choices the following spring.

Rule #32: _____

Be Prepared For Your MIL
To Wear Lots of Perfume

You might be the type that has a fragrance allergy. As soon as you were married, you had your husband dispense with all bottles of scented aftershaves, deodorants and musks. You are rash and headache free—that is—until your MIL comes to visit! She may not know about your hypersensitivity, and you may be reluctant to mention it either. Plus, she really enjoys her perfume, so who are you to deprive her of her trademark scent? So, strategy aside, simply say, "Wow, you smell great, Mom—what IS that perfume you're wearing?" "White Diamonds!" she'll proclaim proudly as you down a couple o' Extra Strength Excedrin. Get yourself an Air Purifier and run it in on HIGH when your MIL comes to stay. Make sure to buy her some chocolate chip cookies for her drive home, and when she finally departs, go soak in a colloidal oatmeal bath to relax yourself back to health!

(At Her House)

Rule #33: _____

Compliment The Way Your
MIL Keeps Her House

Tell your MIL how much you admire her spotless abode—there is nothing that a domestic engineer enjoys hearing more than how nicely she keeps her domain. And it's true—you really can eat off the floors!

Rule#34: _____

Say Nice Things About Your MIL's Cooking

Even if your MIL boils pasta so long that it resembles mashed potatoes, say how delicious it is, and certainly don't bother to mention that you'd rather have it al dènte. Hey, mashed potatoes can be great! Ask her to write down exactly how she makes her sauce. Have your husband get in on the action as well, and make a point of having him whip up a batch next time Mom comes for a visit. Just make sure you pay close attention at the grocery store so that you don't accidentally buy the Contadina instead of the REDPACK!

Rule #35: _____

Do The Dishes When Visiting Your MIL

For this your MIL will most certainly be appreciative. Just make sure you take notice as to *exactly* how she stacks her dishwasher and in what direction to place the silverware—forks and spoons up, knives down.

Rule #36: _____

Always Make the Bed When Staying With Your MIL

This is important to do whenever you're visiting anyone, of course, but especially essential at your MIL's place. And don't forget to strip the sheets and pillowcases, and be sure to fold the blankets neatly on the bed upon your departure.

Rule #37: _____

Be Prepared to Be Enticed By Lots Of Sugary Tempations When Visiting Your MIL

You have recently committed to losing that last ten pounds. You have successfully removed all sugary temptations from your pantry and have implemented an exercise plan you have been adhering to rigorously. However, when you arrive for a visit and your MIL strictly exclaims, "No diets allowed *here*!" enthusiastically reply with, "Oh, I just LOVE that rule!" and you truly do! After all, when in Rome...! There are cookies, cakes and candy on every table, pudding in the fridge and ice cream in the freezer. Also, your MIL may very well further sabotage your efforts by pushing her delights with a breezy, "Have some colachi!" or, "You just *have* to try this cheesecake!" several times a day. The aroma of popcorn wafts through the house and bowls of chips are distributed after the evening meal. It takes an automaton to maintain a healthy regimen in a war zone such as this— so you don't! But, as soon as you start downing those sweet treats Mom will perchance bring it to your attention like so: "Oh, I noticed you didn't touch the [Nonfat] yogurt I bought for you. Humph, no one eats that @#$%^& around here. I guess I'll just have to throw it out then!" leaving you feeling guilty for squandering food and money as well as ashamed you were so weak in your resolve. Instead, approach your trip with a plan of attack. Throw a set of five-pound weights in the car and do a small amount of resistance training daily. Bring your sneakers and take a long walk in the mall to burn off those extra calories you've accumulated. Mostly, don't beat yourself up, and just get back on track as soon as you return home.

Rule #38: _____

...but Make Sure You Don't Give In to All of Them!

So, you have a perfume allergy... surprise, surprise! You may also have the type of sensitive skin whereby you can't even *look* at a chunk of chocolate without breaking out in lumpy-like hives that fester for weeks. You have honed the intricate art of self-restraint and learned to substitute other sweets such as vanilla ice cream and strawberry frozen yogurt in its place. But your MIL may furnish you with fudge the moment you step through her door. As unobjectionably as possible, politely decline, gently explaining its dire detriments to your epidermis to which she may then declare, "That's just a silly old wives' tale! Chocolate doesn't give you pimples! It's because you keep picking your face is why all those zits are all over your chin like that—that's why your skin is such a @#$%^&* *mess*!" Well, it's true, you *do* pick at your face at times of high stress... However, temptation aside, don't let Mom make you prove her wrong about the chocolate! Rather soothe her with a sweet, "Oh, silly me—more likely it's psychosomatic. I'm *so* impressionable that way—I can't believe how sensitive I am!" Then quickly excuse yourself to use the loo. Whew! You have just successfully avoided an eruption of mount Vesuvius on your visage with your award-winning will power. Secretly congratulate yourself on your creamy complexion, then later go to the mall and have yourself a banana and blueberry smoothie at Starbucks!

Rule#39: _____

Be Aware That Your MIL's Mood May Be Directly Affected by The Weather and Act Accordingly

First thing in the morning, at the slightest hint of a cloud your MIL may possibly pronounce, "What a disgusting waste of an excuse for a day! I feel like @#$%^&—I ain't goin' NOWHERE today!" and then proceed to plop herself down in front of the tube for the next eight to ten hours with an expressionless glare. Try to remember that even you yourself have been guilty of judging a day by its drizzle at times. And hey, everyone needs an excuse to veg out once in a while! Simply let Mom be and try not to bother her... best strategy is to tiptoe through the tulips until the sun peeks through the clouds (at which point only your shadow will be at risk!).

Rule #40: _____

Don't Try To Be Environmentally Conscious When Visiting Your MIL

After a shower, do put your towels in the hamper, as you've noticed that your MIL views them as dirty after just one use. For example, while trying to conserve energy you may casually mention that she needn't immediately remove them from the guest bathroom, as you would gladly reuse them for the duration of your visit. To this she may likely respond with, "That would be gross!" So, no worries—let Mom do the laundry and enjoy the luxury of freshly washed towels. The local water tower can handle a few extra loads to be sure!

Rule#41: _____

...but Be As Conservative As Possible When It Comes to TP!

If you're not careful, you may accidentally use too much toilet paper and your MIL's old-fashioned plumbing may get plugged. "Now I have to change the @#$%^&* SEAL!" she'll bewail. So. Follow green-minded celeb Sheryl Crow and only use a single square each time you go.

Rule #42: _____

Hide All Toiletries When
Visiting Your MIL

Make sure you conceal all cosmetics when staying with your MIL, especially if she is expecting company. Even though they may be assiduously organized, she may take it upon herself to place your assortment of gels, cleansers and other amenities under the vanity on a daily basis. Avoid this recurring routine by making a policy of taking your toiletry bag out of the guest bathroom after use and storing it in your suitcase.

Rule #43: _____

Don't Let Your MIL Know
It's That Time Of the Month

Wrap up your feminine care products (even if they are only of the daily protection variety) before throwing them in the receptacle, and always empty the basket in the guest facility after a shower or *you will most likely hear about it*! You see, sometime between going back and forth between the bedroom (getting dressed) and the bathroom (doing your hair) your MIL may appear for inspection. There she will discover your disposables before you've had a chance to empty the refuse, prompting the exclamation, "Would you *please* wrap up your pads *before* throwing them in the garbage? It kind of grosses you out." Simply reply with an apologetic, "Oh my gosh—I can't believe I did that! That is just *too* disgusting!" Bring some small plastic bags, enclose them tightly inside and deposit in the main trash where she will not see them, making sure to never let Mom catch a glimpse of your intimate items again.

(On Dining)

Rule #44: _____

Steer Clear of Religion and Politics When Dining With Your MIL

L oaded topics like politics and religion should be avoided at all costs when you're dining with your MIL. If Mom happens to make some attention-grabbing comment, however, keep your mouth zipped and ask her to pass the salad. Find out exactly how many parts oil to vinegar she uses for the dressing, and marvel at the fact that she never has need for a measuring cup!

Rule#45: _____

Never Let Your MIL Know that You've Enjoyed a Drink (Casual or Otherwise)

Your MIL may love to tell the tale about how in her day she used to go down to the local bar and shoot pool and drink lots of beer. Even if you've heard the legend many times before, act as if it is the first and make sure to throw in something complimentary such as how much you take pleasure in that delightful glass of red Zinfandel every so often. But don't be surprised if she fires back with a disapproving, "So now you're a @#$%^ *alcoholic*, are you?" Therefore, it is always best to let Mom be the one to brag about the beer!

Rule#46: _____

Happily Go Along With Your MIL's Plans

Somehow, everyone in the house seems to know about the daily goings on—*except* for you. A case in point: You notice that the regular pot of sauce is not boiling on the stove. Thinking you might be of some assistance you timidly inquire, "Would you like *me* to cook tonight, Mom?" to which she may then declare, "We're goin' out—we *talked* about it, you know!" Yes, well, okay, she may have indeed talked about it, with everyone other than *you,* that is! Don't expect to be privy to your MIL's plans, and certainly don't get upset. Just smile and say, "Oh, what a lovely idea!" and make sure you fill up on a few healthy snacks before piling into the car for an evening meal at APPLEBEES. (They have a great salad bar, you know!) Throw a container of Tic Tacs in your purse so you can surreptitiously offer Mom a minty treat on the way home. She may decline, but at least roll down the windows so that the flood of family flatulence can freely flee!

Rule #47: _____

Avoid Flatulating Around Your MIL

But if you do accidentally let one escape, your MIL may start waving her hand back and forth furiously in front of her nose, while making the most contorted facial expressions that you have ever seen—rivaling the reflections in the most distorted fun-house mirrors—accompanied by an ear-splitting, "OH MY GOD, OH MY GOD! THAT IS SOOOOO DISGUSTING! Was that *you*, [insert your name here]?" Apologize profusely, and quickly exit the area while covering your face in your hands, affecting the most horror and shame you can possibly muster. Then, try to hold it in the next time Mom is within the radius of a football field. And just to be on the safe side, stock up on some BEANO and get into the habit of using it generously when eating your fruits and veggies!

(On Listening)

Rule #48: _____

Make Sure You Give Your MIL Your Full Attention When She's Telling Stories ... and Restrain the Urge to Interrupt

You may find yourself sitting around with your MIL when abruptly she starts to pontificate about some strangely scary skills—and she can barely contain her enthusiasm! Like so:

"I like to go down the mountains, sit around, drink beer, and shoot targets. I like to shoot a 22—I grew up with that stuff—huntin' and fishin'—I loooove to go huntin'! I shot a squirrel once. I had to skin and cook the darn thing too. I darned ate it too! Now, if you're gonna hunt a deer you're gonna clean it too! That buck shot—those things are hard to get out. And once you get the guts out you can hang that thing. Then you can take it to the local place there and they'll make you deer steak. I like that deer jerky—you know that stuff you buy in the sticks? The round, beef jerky. That. Those things are *good*. I really like those. The younger ones are *real* good. You get an old buck and the meat's too tough. When you don't have any money comin' in ya gotta eat *somethin*! That girl down the hair salon—she got a rich boyfriend. She says he's boring and stuff but I says, 'You'd better keep *him* around —he's RICH!' They eat the scorpions now too— they had that on the "Today Show" there. They were crunchy too. They had that other stuff on that one show there too—chocolate covered grasshoppers. I could have caught 'em around here and had some baby ones. We could have soaked 'em in chocolate and ate 'em! I says yeah, I'm as old as I am but I @#$%ˆ@#&* ain't givin' up that stuff *yet*!"

Whatever you do, do not interrupt the flow. Just make up an excuse at dinnertime for why you have no appetite (as you silently suspect that she may have slipped a couple o' crickets into the pasta Fazool).

Rule#49: _____

You May Need To Hone The Art of Tuning Out

Try to avoid particularly long outings with your MIL if possible or she may get edgy and churn out an unending thread of pessimism. Like so:

"Them two guys down the street are *scum* bags— you can't even pass their house without seeing all that @#$%^& cluttering their front lawn. They shouldn't be allowed to own property, I tell ya!" Her scathing soliloquy may continue at the mall: "Jesus Christ! Doesn't that girl look in the mirror when she gets dressed? She has *some nerve* wearing those pants with a waist like that—all those fat rolls hangin' out at the sides—it's *gross!*" And certainly don't count on intermission in the car on the way home: "...and see that row of apartments over there? That guy's a *slum* lord! I heard it's $189 a month not including cable. That's what Mom and Dad need, some @#$%^&* cable! And speaking of Mom, that damn woman doesn't listen to the doctor! I'm gettin' sick and tired of doin' it for her, too. She's gonna run herself right into the grave and it'll serve her right, I say!" And as you sit down for dinner, you practically *pray* for the finale... "...and Britney Spears—she's another train-wreck—they should put *her* ass in *jail*! When she was startin' out she was all naive and innocent and that—then she turned into a TOTAL TRAMP!" And you can then count on the qualified observation of the cuisine too, as in, "This here pizza's *disgusting*! I can't believe they put mayonnaise on it! Wrap it up and give it to Dad—tell him it's cheese."

Deflect Mom's arduous acerbity by tuning her out as you would a long string of monosyllabic pharmaceutical commercials and thank your lucky stars her disapproving invectives are not being aimed at you!

PART 3:
Her Beloved Son

Rule #50: _____

Give Your MIL Regular Updates On Her Son

If your MIL lodges the complaint that she hasn't heard from your husband in days, (even if they speak on a bi-daily basis) tell her how busy he's been doing all sorts of great things such as cleaning the gutters and unclogging the sink. She may still feel personally ignored, but nonetheless proud that her son is doing a "man's work!"

Rule #51: _____

By No Means Criticize Your Husband To Your MIL

E ven if you are especially mad at your mate, do *not* tell your MIL about it. She may not (D'UH!) take your side and you will end up feeling far worse than before. Save your marital gripes for your girlfriends, your own mother, or better yet, your trusty Daughter-in-Law Solutions Worksheet. (Just apply it to your husband!)

Rule #52: _____

Don't Ever, No Matter How Much You Are Tempted, Complain About Your MIL to Your Husband

This is a conversation you will certainly regret. Better not to put him in this position. Your support system will not include your groom, because he is not required to be in the middle nor should he be. Take note of the MIL incidents that trouble you and jot them down. Make sure you do this when your man is not around or it will invariably spark an argument which is exactly what you are striving to avoid at all costs. Better yet, re-read *The Daughter-in-Law Rules*!

Rule#53: _____

Never Let Your Husband Catch You Imitating Your MIL'S Voice

It is good form to refrain from doing this at all—but if you accidentally slip up, it cannot be stressed enough how important it is not to let your better half overhear you doing so. He will absolutely not appreciate nor find humor in it. If you must, simply save the impressions for your Tuesday night comedy improv class!

Rule #54: _____

Offer to Let Your MIL Have Your Husband Help Her In Times of Need

If your MIL has to have surgery or any kind of operation, offer to send your husband to stay with her for as long as she needs him, otherwise she may beat you to the punch: "When I get my operation, I told that son of mine that he'd better get his skinny butt over here for a couple of nights or so!" This is surely the time for you to do away with any and all objections, and really rally for her rapid recovery. "But of COURSE Mom! He should stay as long as you need him!" you'll respond, and truly mean it. Be sure to refrain from offering up any medical opinions, however. Because if you dare to even delicately broach the benefits of alternative, non-invasive treatments, she may very well react like so: "We're not foolin' around with THAT @#$%^&*—we're going STRAIGHT to the SURGEON!" Best to let Mom make all medical assessments.

PART 4:
Before and After the Baby

What to Expect When You (and Your MIL) are Expecting

Rule#55: _____

Tell Your MIL You Can't Wait to Have Babies

If after only a few weeks of marriage your MIL breaks down wailing, "The only thing I want is grandchildren! I'm the *only* person in [insert her state here] without grandchildren!" smile coyly and tell her that you're already working on it. She will be hard-pressed not to picture you and her son having relations, (don't think of a pink elephant, okay?) and she will most likely not ask you again... at least for the next couple of months, that is!

Rule #56: _____

Allow Your MIL to Share
In Your Pregnancy Joy

As soon as you announce your pregnancy your MIL may certainly jump up and down, run around the house while her eyes well up with tears and holler, "I've waited *so long* for this! I can't believe we're finally pregnant! YIPPIE! I hope it's a boy." Go along with the game and ask her how she's feeling periodically. Offer to bring her water and crackers, slippers and other comforts of home especially during her first trimester.

Rule #57: _____

Let Your MIL "One-Up You" On Things

If you're feeling particularly tired during pregnancy your MIL may tender reflections as such: "When I was nine months pregnant I was on my hands and knees scrubbing the floors! I was out every night at this party and that—*nothing* could keep *me* in. I was *always* on the go!" Of course 30 years ago she was 22 (you are 35) she gained a mere 20 pounds (you gained 60) and she didn't have to go to work everyday. Just say that you wish you had her energy and stamina!

Rule #58: _____

Ask Your MIL To Come Up With Names For Your Unborn Child

If while awaiting results regarding the sex of your impending infant your MIL promptly announces, "As soon as you know what it is, let me know so I can start coming up with names!" say, "Great! I can't wait to see your list!" Then, curl up with the latest version of the All-Time Greatest Baby Name Book and pick your own, of course! But make sure you let Mom supply your peanut with plenty of hypocorisms when he or she arrives and use them copiously in her presence.

Rule #59: _____

Mention Your Concern About The Cats Smothering the New Baby

You already know what to do with the litter, ladies. But regarding your furry friends, while showing your MIL sonogram pics she may pronounce (as per the old wives tale) that you should rid your home of your felines, as they will surely smother the baby to death! Assure Mom that you've already looked into adoptive homes. When your seedling arrives, however, feel free to rescue another kitty from the shelter. (Just make sure the cats don't end up sleeping on your baby's head, though!)

The Happiest
Mother-in-Law On the Block
(Baby's First Year)

Rule #60: _____

Dress Your Newborn Immediately With Outfits From Your MIL

E ven if you've just had a C-section and are suffering from postpartum depression and sleep deprivation, open gifts from your MIL pronto or she may misunderstand and exclaim tearfully, "I guess you don't want any of those clothes I bought for the baby—I guess I'll just give them to *so-and-so's* baby then!" Rather make sure you go through the bag of adorable gear right away, thanking her profusely while ooohing and ahhhing and ask her to dress the tot, suggesting the small pink onesie with flowers or the blue one with a bow, but then again, you can't decide because they are all just soooo cute!

Rule #61: _____

Cover Up While Nursing Around Your MIL

If you choose to breast-feed, your MIL may constantly say things like, "Cover up!" or "Oh, I could *never* do that—I would be SO embarrassed!" If she does catch you in the act you can simply say, "Oh I *totally* agree! It's *so* demoralizing when my child gets hungry and cries, and I have to feed her right there in a public place. I'm training her to take a bottle so that when I'm out and about I won't have to expose myself—it's just *soooo* exhibitionist!" Then happily continue to nourish your bambino wherever and whenever she is hungry, of course! But if you do happen to be out shopping with Mom, make sure to have appropriate paraphernalia for concealing all parts of the epidermis north of the navel, should you need to nurse on a moment's notice.

Rule #62: _____

Lament the Fact That You Didn't Give Breastfeeding a Try

If you ARE a solid bottle-feeding mom, however, your MIL will inevitably make comments such as, "I thought nowadays they say *breast-feeding* is better for the baby. There are those vitamins in there that are just not available in formula. It's just *such* a shame you didn't give it a try..." to which you can then respond, "That is just so true—I'm SO regretful about that! I just hope the baby doesn't get sick from the Enfamil. As well, I was *really* looking forward wearing those special bras and pumping with those cool looking machines... I always get remorseful when I see other moms nursing at the park, or in restaurants. They just lift up their shirts anywhere and VOILA! They are just sooooo lucky!"

Rule #63: _____

Let Your MIL Diaper Your
Baby As Much As She Wants

When your MIL comes to visit and takes over as is her wont, let her! Don't criticize or take issue with her diapering skills, even if she puts them on inside out and backwards. (After all, it's been more than a few years, no?) So, the baby goes around for an hour or two with a wedgie—oh well! Let your MIL smear a half tube of Destin on your duckie's apple cheeks. So, they'll be extra soft, no worries! Luxuriate by telling yourself you're at a spa and give yourself a break. Go out and get a manicure/pedicure—maybe even a massage—you deserve it!

Rule #64: _____

Inform Your MIL You Can't Wait To Have Another Baby

Feel free to do this rule only if your MIL has expressed a desire for more grandchildren. For example, if your twinkle toes has yet to shed her umbilical chord, your MIL may nonetheless put in an application for a new addition such as, "I can't *wait* until she has a little brother or sister to play with!" Say how eager you are to have another. Smile coyly and mention that you're already working on it.

Rule #65: _____

Tell Your MIL You Can't Wait To Stop Breastfeeding

If your MIL asks how long you're going to nurse, say that you'd like to wind it up as soon as possible and that you're going through the weaning process presently. Tell her you're eager to discontinue so that you can get your body back. Then attend La Leche meetings until your child is four (or however long it may take). Don't let Mom know that you are such a softie that you just don't have the heart to actually say no to your privileged puffball. However, when you and the baby are finally good and ready, hellooooooooo, sippy cup!

Rule #66: _____

Call Your MIL and Have the Baby Make Sounds Over the Phone

If you've never heard the sound of uncontainable laughter emanating from your MIL's lips, do this rule. You won't believe your ears as she will giggle and guffaw, chuckle and chortle, snigger, snort, snicker, hoot and cackle away to her heart's delight. May as well record this two-way conversation. This is a rare moment that you would be remiss not to capture!

Rule #67: _____

Allow Your MIL To Use Any Nicknames She Wants

If your MIL calls your child by a moniker you don't particularly like, do not make the mistake of taking issue with it. However, should you decide to express your disapproval you can expect a mildly theatrical reply such as: "You just get upset at every cotton little pickin' thing, [*insert your name here*]!" and she may then stomp off dramatically for an hour or two. Before long, your little angel will make her very own opinions on the matter known to Grandma and everyone else within earshot. But until then, let Mom identify your elf however she wants, adding, "Oh, what an endearing pet name—I sure wish *I* had thought of that one!" And then use it a lot when she's around.

Rule#68: _____

Offer To Let Your MIL
Keep Your Baby Overnight

When your MIL broadcasts, "I can't wait until I can have the baby by myself overnight!" gleefully agree—and tell her how much you anticipate this event as well, even if the thought of being away from your snuggle-bunny makes you as anxious as... an accountant in April! However, by the time your child is old enough to actually do such a thing, most likely she will not want to be away from you all night long anyway. This will eliminate any further discussion of said outing. Don't worry, at some point your little chickadee will want to stay with Grandma, and make sure to reassure Mom of this inevitable fact as well. Hey, there will even come a point when you may actually beg your MIL to baby-sit, so that you can finally have that looooooong overdue romantic overnight getaway (even if it is just down the street at the Holiday Inn!).

Rule #69: _____

Try to Trick Your MIL into Chewing Nicorette

Sure, when your husband was little your MIL may have driven from the Midwest to Florida and back in a big blue 1970's Chevrolet Merry Miler Wagon with the windows up, puffing away for three days straight, and you *still* worry about the possible effects of the second-hand smoke 30 years later. (And you certainly don't want her smoking anywhere near the baby!) Therefore, if your MIL is stuck on the habit, make sure to mention every so often that you're concerned about her health: "We sure do want you to be around for [insert your child's name here] wedding, that's all!" Carry a pack of Nicorette gum in your purse and offer her a stick at regular intervals like so: Double-Mint, Mom?"

Curious George and Your
Mother-in-Law
(The Toddler Years)

Rule #70: _____

Have Your Child Call Your MIL Regularly

As soon as your stripling is able to carry on a conversation, dial up your MIL and let the two yack away. When it's time to hang up, quickly tell Mom how much the little one misses her and that you can't wait to see her as well!

Rule #71: _____

Send Lots Of Pictures of Your Kid to Your MIL

Keep your MIL updated on a regular basis. In addition, go to the mall and get one of those customized mugs or Tee shirts with your rising star's picture on it. You can even get calendars done up at Staples with photos on every page, or mount your faves on poster board for special occasions like Mother's Day, a birthday or Christmas.

Rule #72: _____

Spring For Professional Shots of Your Child

Make *lots* of copies (especially ones with the Easter Bunny, Santa Claus, or a Hanukkah Dreidel) and send your MIL several wallet sizes to use like trading cards with her Bingo buds. Otherwise she may exclaim tearfully, "I'm the ONLY person I know who doesn't get professional photographs to hand out to my friends. I guess I'm just going to have to take her to the mall MYSELF!" So, even while providing weekly photos via e-mail and expending hours of your time documenting your dumpling with home videos, spend the extra money at Sears or The Picture People. Mom truly enjoys seeing your bloom in bunny ears with a blue background, holding a giant carrot. And so will you! You may even get bamboozled into buying every image in the book, complete with Sepia hues, flower borders and glam shots with soft-focus feature. So be extra-prepared to whip out your credit card and make sure your package includes the CD-ROM so that you can replicate all of the above on your printer at home as well!

Rule#73: _____

Save Your Child's Original Artwork For Your MIL

ick out some recent drawings or finger paintings and dispatch them to your MIL. However, do not present her with anything that includes traces of your creative input or she may refuse it immediately. For example, if your child's compositions end up resembling things such as puppies or frogs, you may feel compelled to color them in, embellish, and label them as such. Your MIL then might say something like, "*These* aren't *hers*! I won't put *those* up!" Instead, provide Mom with the scribbles alone. These are the ones that will invariably end up framed at her house. "Ahhh, now that's TALENT!" she'll proclaim proudly.

Rule#74: _____

Follow Your MIL's Instructions To a T

If your MIL e-mails you specific items to pack for your tot prior to a visit, be sure to include each and every article even though when you get there she may utter either, "You didn't bring very many clothes for the baby!" or "You *really* do have a tendency to over pack, don't you?" Mom's list may generally refer to specific attire that she has purchased for your pumpkin such as, "Blue Shirt with Butterfly" and "Striped Pants with Heart on Pocket." And the next time you go for a visit, preclude it with a phone call like so: "Ever since I had the baby I've had *such* oatmeal brain! Please email me if there is anything you'd like for me to pack so I don't forget, okay? See ya!" Then hang up quickly before she can fire off an inventory of items as long as the Rio Grande.

Rule #75: _____

Let Your MIL Dress Your Kid The Way She Wants To

If your MIL tells you your child looks homeless as she never wears anything that matches, coincide immediately and agree that you've been terribly mortified since your Muppet has recently insisted on picking out her own wardrobe. Then let your MIL select an outfit, but suppress all chuckles when she tries to get your itinerant into the coordinating Baby Gap ensemble! As well, at the slightest sight of any extraneous strand of string straying off a shirt certainly be prepared for Mom to pronounce, "Look at that dress! It's *shredded*! That is going straight into the JUNK PILE!" Therefore, make sure to sew all errant hemlines before packing any of your fluffy fawn's favorites.

Rule #76: _____

Have Your MIL Bathe Your Foundling

Upon arrival at your MIL's, be prepared for her to drag your ragamuffin to the bath as if she has never seen a dirt-free day in her life. (Okay, so you got busy the last couple of days!) Take the opportunity to relax in front of the 50-inch super-high definition TV with surround sound and kick back in the La-Z-Boy while you're at it!

Rule#77: _____

Make Sure Your Offspring Sleeps In PJ's When Visiting Your MIL

Now, as it may be summer, your little Care Bear may have gotten into the habit of sleeping in her T-shirt and shorts. Your MIL may behave as if she doesn't perceive you properly. "Are you saying that you don't have pajamas for her? What in *God's* name is she going to sleep in, her *birthday suit*? She can't sleep in her clothes! They're FILTHY!" Simply harmonize with Mom like so: "Oh my gosh, you're right! I can't believe I didn't pack pajamas—I'm going to have to run out to JCPenney tomorrow to buy her a couple of pairs! For tonight, though, how about we let her sleep in this clean pair of shorts and this soft T-shirt? She'll probably be *terribly* uncomfortable... I certainly hope she makes it through the night! We'll have to make sure she gets a good long nap tomorrow, that's for sure." At least now you'll have a nifty excuse to meander the mall the next day!

Rule#78: _____

Stay Away From Highfalutin Vocabulary Around Your MIL

If you are styling your daughter's hair, your MIL may perchance ask what the @#$%^ you are doing to which you might innocently reply, "Making tendrils!" Mom then may very likely exclaim, "Speak English, [Insert your name here]!" Better to stick to simpler language such as curls or waves.

Rule#79: _____

Say How Much You Love The Way Your MIL Does Your Child's Hair

On the other hand, if your MIL styles your daughter's hair, make sure to say just how adorable it looks. Do not redo it or she might sarcastically blurt out, "Oh, I guess I didn't do her hair right, then!" leaving you feeling like the cat that ate the bird. Your cockatoo looks cute no matter what, so unless your little one complains about it herself, keep the ` do in. Hey, you might even try a similar thing yourself the next time. After all, brushed hair with barrettes never goes out of style!

Rule #80: _____

Let Your MIL Feed Your Child What She Wants When Visiting

If you notice your MIL bestowing Wonder Bread with butter on your little bottomless pit a few times a day, just remember that your husband eventually grew up and seems to be in relatively good health. Although you may feel frustrated and be compelled to suggest, "I would prefer if you didn't feed her that stuff at *every* meal, okay?" better to let your MIL indulge your child's requests for the nutritionally devoid foodstuffs. Otherwise your kid will soon come crying, "Grammy said that *you* said that I can't have white bread with butter ANYMORE!" forcing you to relent sheepishly, "Well, she can have it at least *once* a day, I guess the stuff won't kill her!" Don't make a federal issue out of it, as your pipsqueak will eventually be back to eating apples and whole-wheat bagels upon Mom's departure!

Make Sure To Clean up
Carefully At Your MIL's

*A*fter feeding your fledgling at your MIL's, make sure you polish the tiles until they shine like a pearl or she may very well rebuke, "This here @#$%^&* is all *over* the damn place!" while pinpointing a tiny piece of potato on the linoleum floor. Make sure your Lilliputian makes a concerted effort as well, or Mom may then reprove, "You come and pick these here straw things up RIGHT now or I'm putting them straight in the BURN PILE!" Now, granted, once in a while it's nice to have someone other than yourself be the bad guy in the game of clean up with your cub. But, this is the stuff nightmares are made of—"Burn Piles?" Straws never to be sucked through again? *Yikes*! Help your mini mess-maker straighten up pronto and then take a nice trip to Mickey D's for a special treat (and throw a couple o' extra straws in your purse for a rainy day— Ronald won't mind!)

Rule #82: _____

Save Every Toy Your MIL Gives Your Tot For at Least Four Seasons

Your MIL is always excited to make a trip to Toys"R"Us to scope out the latest up-to-the-minute, gargantuan primary-colored objects for her precious grandkid's holiday booty. She spends mucho bucks each Christmas on the newest "Strawberry Shortcake Deluxe Cowgirl Adventure Set" or the "Dancing Princesses Enchanted Melodies Furniture" or the "Barbie Let's Get Ready Vanity With Make-Up Included!" And your baby pigeon is in seventh heaven, naturally! At least until she opens the container. Soon after the toy is unfastened, (taking you several minutes to unravel the Fort Knox-like wires and thief-proof packaging), she'll most likely just end up tossing the doll to the side, jumping gloriously into the box leaving the plastic monstrosity sorrowfully ignored, never to be played with again. But nevertheless, your MIL so enjoys her buying sprees, and you certainly appreciate her generosity, so let her! As well, take care to ensure that the playthings are front and center upon Mom's arrival and make sure you yourself engage in some agriculture play with the latest "Dora the Explorer Gardening Pack." Hey, you may even acquire a green thumb!

Rule #83: _____

Don't Feel Guilty For Not Having Lost the Baby Weight Yet

After the birth of your babe, your MIL may now and then buy you clothes that are two sizes too small. Although you are fully aware of that last 20 pounds you've been carrying around since D-day, now that it's summer, you are currently employed as a full-time cruise director, activity planner, sous-chef, stylist, personal shopper, chauffeur, hairstylist, tailor, doctor, photographer, party-planner, swim instructor, opponent, answering service, costume designer, pet-sitter, book reader, hand-holder and poopy-diaper changer (*31 Uses for a Mom*, anyone?)! You should be going to that GYM and dieting yourself silly, so that you can be the "Posh Mom" that is all the new rage. Hmmm, not sure about *that* one! Simply thank your MIL profusely for the gifts, while visualizing yourself looking slim and trim in that new sweater set with cinch-waist belting. Then, if you happen to

dig into that container
beckons every time y
freezer, just enjoy yours
small for long, and you
array of yoga and Pil
know it!

There's a Wocket In Your
Mother-in-Law's Pocket!
(The Preschooler)

Rule #84: _____

Don't Let Your MIL Make You Feel Badly That Your Three-Year-Old Is Still in Diapers

When you visit your MIL with your preschooler she may possibly comment, "*I* would have had her potty trained by *now. I* wouldn't put up with *that*!" Now, if you're the type to spend a week or two with your little one naked running around the house, following her with wipes or a cup to catch the poop and pee and clean up after her like a puppy, by all means go for it! But, for those of us who are more apt to wait until the child shows some interest, relax in the knowledge that by Kindergarten everyone will be happily outfitted in the latest Little Mermaid or Spiderman undies. Simply reply with a light-hearted, "Oh I *know*! I can't believe she's still in those silly diapers—and we are going absolutely *broke* from buying them at Costco each week! I recently heard about a great method called "Potty Train in a Day" where you show her a dolly that wets, and I just got a copy of *Once Upon A Potty* from the library so we can watch it together nightly. I am *so* tired of changing her—so hopefully she won't be going to High School in diapers!" Then, happily grab your Pampers and Balmex and take your kid to the park for the day, secure in the knowledge that you are not yet dependant on finding pubic facilities on a moment's notice. Of course, when you finally leave your hummingbird for a weekend with Mom, upon your return you sweetly inquire how it went with the potty. "Well, you just can't FORCE her into it, you know!" <SIGH!>

Rule #85: _____

Don't Edit Your Child's Grammar When Your MIL is Around

When your MIL addresses your poppet with Midwestern-speak such as ending sentences with prepositions, (Where you at?) or by leaving out the verb "to be," (This needs cleaned!) remember that your husband grew up and seems to utilize syntax relatively well—that is—at least when you correct him! So, bite your tongue in her presence but when Mom is in the next room and your child announces, "I ate it all gone!" just gently correct her and simply go about your day.

Rule #86: _____

Never Say Negative Things About Your MIL In Front Of Your Child

Your sapling will inevitably repeat it back to her, *and you will regret it!* By all means, have the conversation about how eating good food promotes heath and radiance, but leave out the part where you say "...unlike Grandma who sometimes eats unwholesome things and then looks unwell." You will *pray* that your child will not remember what just slipped out. FAT CHANCE! The next time she's on the phone with Grandma she will promptly announce, "Mommy says you eat bad food and look *really sick*!" Train yourself to say only polite things about your children's grandmother, or anyone else for that matter, in front of them.

Rule #87: _____

Be Tolerant If Your MIL Isn't Familiar With Your Religious Background

You want your child to be exposed to your religion as well as your husband's, so you may bring a Menorah to light on Chanukah while visiting. Try not to act incredulous when your MIL queries, "What's *that* thing?" So there are no Jews in the Midwest, it's not her fault!

Rule #88: _____

Avoid Discussing Event Planning With Your MIL

When undertaking an affair such as your child's birthday bash, refrain from expressing anxiety about the details involved or your MIL may possibly make a subtlety sour aside such as, "*Your* party, not mine!" If the topic does come up simply say something like, " What was I *thinking*? I'm *so* crazy for doing this. I hope it's not going to be an absolute *disaster*!" Then promptly change the subject by sliding in with a shifty sleight-of-hand, "Oh my God!" Did you hear what [famous celebrity] so-and-so has done now?"

Rule #89: _____

Ask Your MIL's for Tips On Child Rearing

Your MIL may occasionally witness your little Barbie Princess having the occasional meltdown and declare, "She doesn't act like this when she's with *me*. She's like night and day. *I* wouldn't put up with *that* kind of behavior! When [insert your husband's name here] was little he tried that on me once in a store and I pulled his pants down and gave him the biggest public whoopin' you EVER seen. You can bet that he never pulled that on *me* again! You know what you need—you need the SUPERNANNY!" Simply say, "Oh, you're *so* right—please give me strategies on how to be a stricter mother!" But not to worry. As soon as Mom leaves, your little rascal will surely revert back to her well-behaved angelic ways (at least for the next couple of hours, that is!).

Rule #90: _____

Refrain From Discussing the Origins of Meat (or anything about your vegetarian leanings) with Your Moppet While In the Presence of Your MIL

If your MIL is defrosting raw hamburger in the kitchen, your curious cub may creep up to the counter and innocently conjecture, "Is that worms? Does that come from a pig? Is that dead animal flesh?" As you gently enlighten her that it in fact comes from a cow, your MIL may then add in her own two cents on the matter like so: "It's PROTEIN! It's good for you and you need it to grow!" which alas, doesn't seem to satisfy your inquisitive imp's interest and she charges forth with the energy of an electric eel like so: "Why? Why do you eat dead cows? WHY?" Do your best to resist adding something of your own to the effect of, "But you can also get protein from other sources as well such as beans and rice, kernels and seeds, vegetables, grains, cheese, yogurt and milk!" But beware—should you choose this route you may surely suffer the silent treatment for the better part of the afternoon, and very well into the evening hours, and possibly for the next decade or two as well. Rather, concur with a conciliatory, "Oh yes, Grandma's right. Protein is absolutely necessary for a growing girl!" Then, grab a handful of nuts and offer one to your offspring like so: "An almond, dear?"

(On Work and Feminism)

Rule #91: _____

Let Your MIL Think That You Don't Work

uring a second pregnancy your MIL might pronounce, "You're lucky that you don't have to *work*!" And although it's true that you may not have a traditional 9-5, (you might be a musician, artist or writer in addition to being a full-time mother) you may be tempted to stick up for the full-time job of motherhood and retort, "So, taking care of two children isn't *work*?" to which she may then respond, "You don't have *two* children!" at which point you will certainly be silenced as technically she is correct (although you are due the following Tuesday). Rather save your energy for D-day and declare, "You are *so* right, Mom. It is *such* a blessing not to have to go to an office everyday. I just *love* to lounge around in the morning, and enjoy my daughter 'round the clock. I am soooo lucky!" And you know, it's true—if you are fortunate enough to be able to afford to stay home and raise your kids, (if you want to, that is), count your blessings!

Rule #92: _____

Don't Let Your MIL Make You Feel Guilty For Working

If you do work full-time, your MIL might consistently state such gems as, "It's *such* a shame that you can't stay home! I would *never* let someone else raise *my* child!" to which you will reply, "I know! I just HATE that I have to go to the daily grind. It makes me feel *so* guilty leaving my cherub to play with all those kids. I'm sure she's absolutely miserable! She really dislikes finger painting and being outside all day. I'm thinking of quitting. As a matter of fact, I've already looked into severance packages!" Then get that promotion and take your family to Disney World on your next vacay. And make sure to bring Mom back a Mickey Mouse T-shirt or two!

Rule #93: _____

Realize That Your MIL is Not a Feminist By Nature

You may casually mention that you've already started a college fund for your child. Instead of expecting your MIL to be proud and lavish you with praise for your foresight and ability to save for such a wonderful cause so far in advance, be prepared that Mom might instead counter with, "Well, she may not *want* to go to college! She may just want to stay home and be a MUMMY!" So, instead of going into your feminist schpiel on the importance of education—what with the myriad choices available for wonderful careers, why in earth's name would your daughter settle for such a lot in life? say instead, "That's true, she might! Well, whatever makes her smile is alright with me!" and leave it at that.

(When the Second Baby
Arrives)

Rule #94: _____

Avoid Comparing Your Children In Front Of Your MIL

S hould you make an innocent remark about how different your pups' personalities are, you may let slip something to the effect of, "This baby is so much calmer and more mellow than the first one, who was hyperactive and never sat still for a moment!" Your MIL might then bounce back without missing a beat, "That's because that's how YOU were, of course. Babies pick up on *everything,* you know." Have a super-snappy, conciliatory comeback meticulously prepared: "Oh, I agree! I was *such* a hyper first-time mother—I had no idea WHAT I was doing and I was a *complete* mess! I'm absolutely *sure* that our daughter could feel every nervous bone in my body. It's a good thing that [insert your husband's name here] was around to calm me down or the white-coats would have put me in a straight jacket and performed a frontal lobotomy. Thank God *one* of us is levelheaded and calm around here. We wouldn't want our kids to grow up acting like their crazy mom, now, would we?"

Rule #95: _____

During Bad Weather, Call Your MIL to Reassure Her That Her Grandkids are Fine

Your MIL will most likely be the first to call and inform you of the latest natural disaster that has been looming in your region. For example: the phone rings and she may announce in a panic-stricken tone, "I saw on TV that there was a tornado in your area— the first one in 118 years! Did you stock the cellar? How are the kids? Tell me you've prepared the cellar! You HAVE prepared the cellar, haven't you? I keep tellin' that son of mine to keep extra batteries down there. What is WRONG with him? And what about those extra blankets I brought you? The kids might be cold. You'd better have kept those blankets!" After calmly explaining that the little ones are safe and sound and although you had a bit of rain there was nothing out of the ordinary going on weather-wise she still may surely opine, "Well! You better rush them down to the basement if you get wind of a hurricane warning. You can't play with their lives you know—no sense takin' any chances!" Now, your MIL may have lived in the Midwest with a subterranean vault that she has been running to for years in fear of the dreaded twister upon the slightest hint on the Weather Channel. Meanwhile, you live in or near a cosmopolitan city that has barely seen a flood, much less a cyclone! Coolly reply that you are so glad that she has such expertise in this subject, and assure her that you have adequately stocked the underground room with the requisite bottles of water, cans of food, flashlight, blankets and batteries. Let Mom know that you will call her the minute you hear about the impending typhoon and oops, you have to go—the baby needs changing!

Rule #96: _____

Refrain From Discussing the Irresponsible Traits of Babysitters With Your MIL

You may be lamenting about how hard it is to find reliable help these days, and just how frustrating it is to hire a baby-sitter, only to have her cancel at the last minute. Your MIL may then quip, "You gave birth to those kids, *too bad*! You should have thought of that *before* you had 'em!" Agree with her with a solid, "Yes, you are *absolutely* right about that. I should never expect to depend on anyone but myself to take care of my own children. It's a lucky thing that those young girls are even *considering* watching our little monsters once in a while. I'm so grateful for whatever help I can get, even if it's every so often, now and then." Then, erase the number of the negligent teen from your database, and find someone you can count on come hell or high water!

Rule #97: _____

...but Don't Expect Your MIL to Baby-sit for You Either!

So, babysitters are unreliable—what else is new? Therefore, when you are about to go visit your MIL for a few days with the kids, you get especially excited when she offers her services! "Well, you two can go out to the movies if you'd like. You'd might as well take advantage of me while you're here," she may reasonably relay, to which you enthusiastically rejoin, "Mom, that's a *wonderful* idea! As much as you're willing to watch the kids, we sure would love to go out at least a couple of times while we're there, so thank you so much for the offer!" to which she may then retort with lightening speed, "Well! We'll just have to see. I can't promise I'll be up for it—we'll just have to play *that* one by ear." SIGH! Don't forget that she has been taking extra meds for that arthritis in her neck so be extra sure to be as helpful as possible when you arrive. Plan on renting some flicks from the local video store (and con the gremlins into going to bed super early). Just make sure it's something your MIL enjoys as well—anything with Brad Pitt should do the trick!

Rule #98: _____

Don't Be Surprised If Your MIL's Motherly Advice is Then Followed By a Magic Charm

So, your MIL has finally agreed to watch the kids so that you can go out for the evening. Before leaving the house she may caution, "Better take a sweater with you—those theaters sure do get cold!" Just as you are about to thank her profusely for having just taken your comfort factor into consideration, she may then sew it up with a sobering, "I sure do hope you get hot flashes! I started gettin' 'em just about around the age you are now. I can't wait for you to finally know how I feel—like &^*@#$#$% CRAP!" Niiiiiiice. As you exit the house, give Mom a speedy squeeze and thank her profusely for kid-sitting. Then go and enjoy the latest Tinseltown comedy for a pick-me-up!

Rule #99: _____

Get Out Of Dodge When The Going Gets Tough

If your MIL seems to be in an especially bad mood and starts throwing off a virulent vibe, take it as an opportunity to suggest that you and your husband get out of her hair by going out for dinner. Of course, your plan might very well be thwarted if Mom shoots back with an icy, "Better take them kids with you—I ain't cookin' *tonight*!" In that case, grab your goblins and take 'em to the mall for pizza and ice cream.

Rule #100: _____

Tell Your MIL You Can't Wait To Have Even *More* Babies

While reminiscing over your budding pre-pubescents' precocious pix, disclose to your MIL just how much you miss those tiny little fingers and toes. Then sigh uncontrollably while deflecting your gaze longingly upward. As a tear trickles down your cheek, mention what a blessing it would be if God would only provide you with just *one more* little angel. Then practice birth control religiously, or natural family planning at the very least. Or, if you're absolutely *certain* beyond a shadow of a doubt that you are done with procreation, have your tubes tied!

PART 5:
Most of All

Rule #101: _____

Do Everything You Can To Make Your MIL Proud

When your MIL finds out you're writing a book about her tell her you're going to make a million bucks. She'll be super-psyched and say, "I know I can be a bitch, Sally! I'm a *Leo*! But you're stubborn too. We're a lot alike, you know! Now, go write a best-seller or I'll kick your butt!"

Final Thoughts _____

Whew! You may feel like lying down after reading all these rules, but don't despair. I promise that the practice of these rules will come naturally once your priorities are in order. The bottom line while you're doing these rules, is to really and truly learn to appreciate your MIL. After all, she did give birth to your husband and you are forever thankful to her for that! So, although there will always be problems because of a general lack of commonalities, goals and cultural pursuits, we just sort of have to give up that fantasy and let our MIL be herself. We must try to always give her the benefit of the doubt, and put our stubborn natures aside, generously sharing her son and the kids happily for the short time we have to be with her. We can all grow much closer to our MIL's through the children!

I leave you with this wish: that you may develop a respectful and loving relationship with your MIL and learn to appreciate her for who she is, where she came from and what she is to become. Take heed to one of the great spiritual laws of success: The quickest way to get what you want is to help others get what they want. Be a loving, kind, generous, openhearted, sensitive person and the world will reflect that back to you—even in the form of your mother-in-law—and she may just surprise you and turn out to be an ally and a friend. Mine certainly did!

Love,
Sally Shields
"The MIL Manager!"

The Daughter-in-Law
Solutions Worksheet

Here is an easy four-step worksheet to help you apply
The Daughter-in-Law Rules to your own particular MIL
situation. The fundamental idea is to jot down all the
things that you do that seem to bother your MIL (and all
the things that your MIL does that bother you) and what
was said at those times. You will then come up with a
rule title and a solution to deal with each and every
troublesome circumstance that arises. This handy
mnemonic will help you remember how to do this:

I   —   Identify the problem

N   —   Note what was said

C   —   Create a rule

S   —   Set up a solution

Identify the problem. In other words, tell your story (i.e. What happened, what you did, what she did)

Note what was said (i.e., what you said, what she said, exact quotes are good here)

Create a rule title. Here are some examples of the ways that you might begin this phrase:

Allow Your MIL, Give Your MIL, Have Your MIL, Inform Your MIL, Let Your MIL, Tell Your MIL, Be Aware That, Be Objective When, Be Prepared For, Be Prepared To, Be Ready To, Be Tolerant If, Better To, Do Everything You Can To, Make Sure To, Offer To, Strive To, Try To, Don't Try To, Try Not To, You May Need To, Don't Be Surprised If, Don't Ever, Don't Let, Do Not Anticipate, Do Not Expect, Do Not Require, Frequently Ask For, Happily Go Along With, Know That, Realize That, Reassure, Refrain From, Stay Away From, Steer Clear Of, etc.

Set up a solution

Formulate your resolution. The objective is to always give your MIL the benefit of the doubt at this point in the process. This comes under the umbrella of good will. However, be aware that you may have to tell your MIL one thing but ultimately do what ever it is that you want or need to do. This comes under the umbrella of self-preservation!

I.N.C.S. for D.I.L.Z.

Remember, you won't be able to prevent hurtful MIL comments and misunderstandings overnight. This is a system that must be developed over time. The trick is to realize that once you have identified a certain area of conflict between you and your MIL, it is likely that the very same situation will surface again. (After all, how many times have you had the same old argument with your husband about something, right?) The goal is to prevent you from having the same old reactions to repeat DIL zings (**D.I.L.Z**). By utilizing the simple I.N.C.S. technique, eventually you will create your own personalized set of rules customized for your very own MIL. This is your ace-in-the-hole because you will then be prepared the NEXT time a similar circumstance occurs. Ultimately, your MIL will be hard-pressed to find anything to complain about (and you might be pleasantly surprised on your end as well). It's fun once you get the hang of it, and you will be amazed when you develop a genuine like for one-another.

Enjoy!

About the Author

Sally Shields is an award-winning pianist, composer, speaker, and author. She graduated with honors from the New England Conservatory and was a recipient of the Boston Jazz Society Award. Winner of the 17th annual Great American Jazz Piano Competition, her articles and transcriptions are featured regularly in *Piano Today Magazine* and her book, *Modern Jazz Piano,* is the standard theory manual for several music programs, including Princeton University. Her children's song "It's Christmastime, Once Again" was a finalist in the John Lennon Songwriting Contest and her music is currently featured on the ABC TV daytime drama *All My Children.* When not traveling and performing around the world—most recently with bestselling author and musician James McBride—Sally (a vegetarian) lives in New York City with her husband (not a vegetarian!) and their two children.

Note: Although the relationship with her MIL was rocky at the outset, with the implementation of the devices outlined in *The Daughter-in-Law Rules*, the two now enjoy a special bond—which got even better, interestingly enough—after her MIL found out she was writing this book!

Also Available by Sally Shields

○ A full-length mp3 download of Sally's deliciously delightful "Moon Melodies" —an hour's worth of soothing solo piano lullabies—assuredly to lull your infant to absolute repose!

"This is a wonderful project with musical heart and soul, having a strong, sincere, universally clear concept with personal artistic integrity. These 17 individual ballads, modeled after Bach's Well-Tempered Clavier provide an hours' worth of pure peacefulness as well as a lifetime of musical pleasure."

Bob Karcy
president, Arkadia Records

○ An mp3 of Sally's original full- length 60 minute CD "Cruisin'!" as heard on ABC TV's "ALL MY CHILDREN!"

"Sally Shields caresses the piano with sensitivity and love, and the colors she uses demonstrate her gift and vision."

McCoy Tyner
four time Grammy winner

○ An mp3 download of Sally's full-length 60 minute CD, "Yes, Indeed!" including the original hit song, "Stay the Same" as performed by vocalist Carolyn Leonhardt (background singer for Steely Dan)!

"In her music, Sally Shields creates a rich aural tapestry. Her compositions and playing are evocative—much like compelling prose, resulting in beauty and soul."

Andy Laverne
editor, New York Times Magazine

○ Sally Shield's Life Transforming Book of Poetry, "A Pond Beneath the Moon" including her award-winning poem!

The editors of The International Library of Poetry are thrilled to inform you that the poem, "A Pond Beneath the Moon" by Sally Shields was honored with the prestigious Editor's Choice Award because of her artistic accomplishments and unique perspective—characteristics found in the most noteworthy poetic works.

Howard Ely
managing editor of Poetry.com

As well: _____

- o   Private Consultations
- o   Speaking Engagements
- o   The DIL Rules Gift Certificates
- o   *The Daughter-in-Law Rules* E-book
- o   The Daughter-in-Law 101 Workshop
- o   Piano Performances available upon request

Every bit of Sally's philosophy is designed to make a profound and positive improvement in your life, intensify your level of happiness and help you live far more peacefully with your husband and MIL!

Please visit Sally on the web at www.TheDILRules.com for contests, giveaways, free bonus gifts, The DIL Rules newsletter, the 44 Top Tips Cheat Sheet, free music ...and more!